ESPORTS

FORTNITE

KENNY ABDO

Fly!
An Imprint of Abdo Zoom
abdobooks.com

abdobooks.com

Published by Abdo Zoom, a division of ABDO, P.O. Box 398166, Minneapolis, Minnesota 55439. Copyright © 2023 by Abdo Consulting Group, Inc. International copyrights reserved in all countries. No part of this book may be reproduced in any form without written permission from the publisher. Fly!™ is a trademark and logo of Abdo Zoom.

Printed in the United States of America, North Mankato, Minnesota.
052022
092022

THIS BOOK CONTAINS RECYCLED MATERIALS

Photo Credits: Alamy, AP Images, Getty Images, Shutterstock, ©BagoGames p.cover / CC BY 2.0, ©Sergey Galyonkin p.9/ CC BY-SA 2.0
Production Contributors: Kenny Abdo, Jennie Forsberg, Grace Hansen
Design Contributors: Candice Keimig, Neil Klinepier

Library of Congress Control Number: 2021950298

Publisher's Cataloging-in-Publication Data

Names: Abdo, Kenny, author.
Title: Fortnite / by Kenny Abdo.
Description: Minneapolis, Minnesota : Abdo Zoom, 2023 | Series: Esports | Includes online resources and index.
Identifiers: ISBN 9781098228477 (lib. bdg.) | ISBN 9781644947838 (pbk.) | ISBN 9781098229313 (ebook) | ISBN 9781098229733 (Read-to-Me ebook)
Subjects: LCSH: Video games--Juvenile literature. | eSports (Contests)--Juvenile literature. | Fortnite Battle Royale (Game)--Juvenile literature. | Epic Games, Inc.--Juvenile literature. | Imaginary wars and battles--Juvenile literature.
Classification: DDC 794.8--dc23

TABLE OF CONTENTS

Fortnite 4

Backstory 8

Journey 14

Glossary 22

Online Resources 23

Index 24

FORTNITE

Fortnite has captured the imaginations of more than 350 million players around the globe!

The game started off with a typical **co-op format**. It went on to change the esports world when it became a **battle royale** title.

BACKSTORY

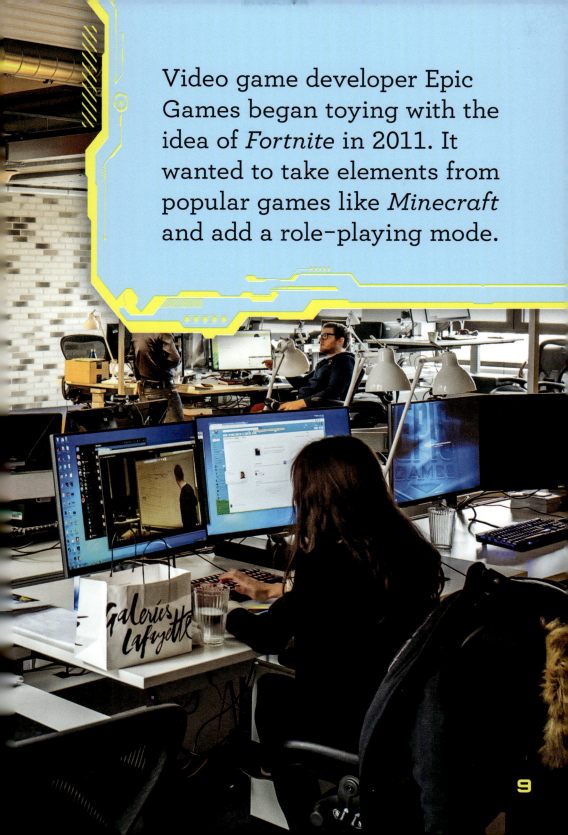

Video game developer Epic Games began toying with the idea of *Fortnite* in 2011. It wanted to take elements from popular games like *Minecraft* and add a role-playing mode.

PlayerUnknown's Battlegrounds (*PUBG*) became a worldwide hit in 2017. Epic wanted to take what it had with *Fortnite* and add **battle royale** gameplay like *PUBG*.

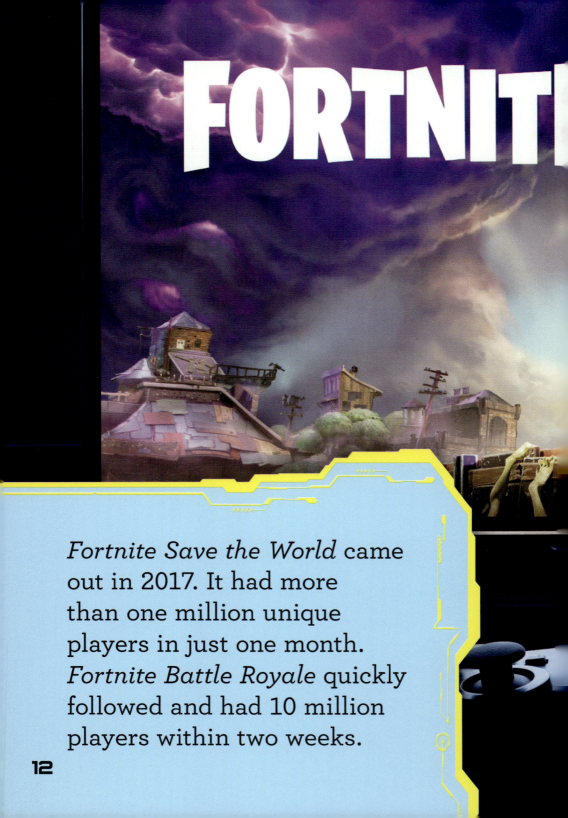

Fortnite Save the World came out in 2017. It had more than one million unique players in just one month. *Fortnite Battle Royale* quickly followed and had 10 million players within two weeks.

JOURNEY

In 2018, famous **streamer** Ninja broke viewer count records. Playing with Travis Scott, Drake, and other celebrities, the superstar stream skyrocketed *Fortnite's* fame.

The first Fortnite Pro-Am competition was held at the 2018 E3 conference. It was won by Ninja and DJ Marshmello. They donated $1 million of the prize money to **charity.**

Later that year, Epic Games began hosting a **Summer Skirmish** series. Each week had a different **format**. A second competition series, the **Fall Skirmish**, shortly followed.

The 2019 Fortnite World Cup was one of the biggest events in esports history. Kyle Giersdorf walked away with $3 million. Just 16 years old at the time, he beat 99 other players!

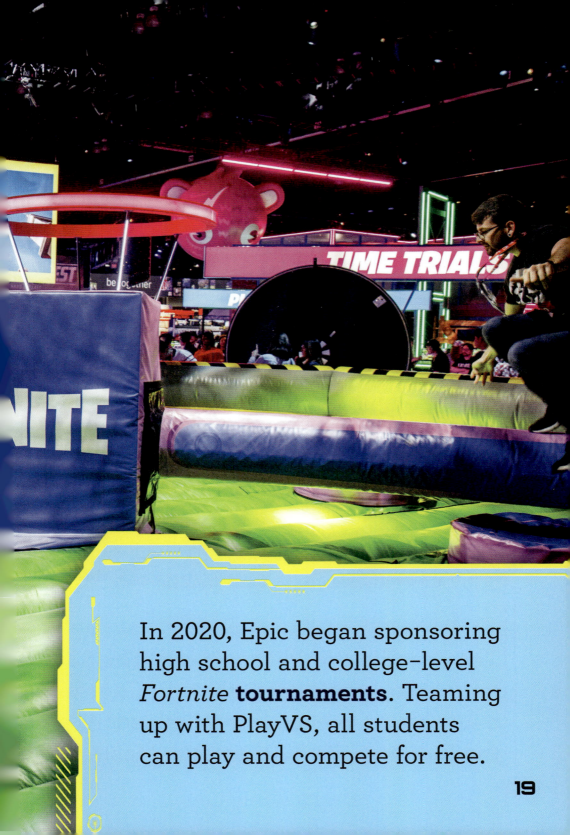

In 2020, Epic began sponsoring high school and college-level *Fortnite* **tournaments**. Teaming up with PlayVS, all students can play and compete for free.

The Fortnite World Cup is big. The $3 million top prize beats the winnings in many major events, like Wimbledon, the Indianapolis 500, and the Masters!

Fortnite has proven to be one of the most successful **battle royale** games in history. And it will continue to **dominate** the esports arena.

GLOSSARY

battle royale – a competition between many participants that goes until there is only one left.

charity – an organization set up to provide help and raise money for those in need.

co-op – short for cooperative, a type of video game that allows players to work together as a team.

dominate – to be much more powerful or successful than others.

Fall Skirmish – a 6-week series of *Fortnite* competitions between September and October.

format – the way a game is set up with rules and guidelines.

streamer – a person who broadcasts themselves in real time while playing video games.

Summer Skirmish – an 8-week series of *Fortnite* competitions between July and September.

tournament – a set of games or matches held to find a first-place winner.

ONLINE RESOURCES

To learn more about Fortnite, please visit **abdobooklinks.com** or scan this QR code. These links are routinely monitored and updated to provide the most current information available.

INDEX

championships 15, 16, 17, 20

DJ Marshmello 15

Drake 14

Epic Games 9, 10, 16, 19

Fortnite Battle Royale (game) 12

Fortnite Save the World (game) 12

Giersdorf, Kyle (player) 17

Indianapolis 500 20

Masters Tournament 20

Minecraft (game) 9

Ninja (player) 14, 15

PlayerUnknown's Battlegrounds (game) 10

PlayVS 19

Scott, Travis 14

Wimbledon 20